Earl Hall

D1377437

NEW ENGLAND
IN COLOR

Profiles of America

NEW ENGLAND

in Color

A Collection of Color
Photographs by
SAMUEL CHAMBERLAIN

With an Introductory Text
and Notes on the Illustrations by
STEWART BEACH

HASTINGS HOUSE · PUBLISHERS

New York, 10016

Second edition January 1971
Third edition December 1971

PUBLISHED 1969 BY HASTINGS HOUSE, PUBLISHERS, INC.

All rights reserved, including the right to reproduce
this book or portions thereof in any form or by any means,
electronic or mechanical, including photo copying,
recording or by any information storage and retrieval system,
without permission in writing from the publishers

Published simultaneously in Canada by
Saunders, of Toronto, Ltd., Don Mills, Ontario

Library of Congress Catalog Card Number: 71–78250
SBN Number: 8038–5013–1

Printed and bound in England by Jarrold and Sons Ltd., Norwich

CONTENTS

That Northeast Corner
of America

I

OUR LAND is so vast and so varied in its contours and its environments that no single book can describe it. To know the country you must absorb it region by region. Quick visits will not do. America is all vacationland now in almost any season. Some sections are more sharply defined than others—by history and tradition and mannerisms that have lingered long after the pioneers first set them in place. Despite the changes that time and expansion and developing industry have made, they still retain the patina of their beginnings. Two such regions on the Eastern Seaboard are Tidewater Virginia—and New England.

In both the mark of our original English heritage is firmly etched, for they are the oldest. New York's settlers were Dutch, but little of that heritage remains except in family genealogies and in place names which have not changed since they were established in the seventeenth century. It was in Virginia and New England that the venturesome Englishmen first planted their colonies, and in both much of visible history remains in houses and churches, old taverns, and other buildings that remember the past, as well as in the land. In rural New England the land itself seems little changed since the last ice cap of the glacier age slowly receded some ten thousand years ago, leaving the sparkling lakes, the rugged mountains, and the bouldered earth that challenged the first farmers to scratch out their crops.

In 1614 Captain John Smith, whose name is forever linked with Jamestown, coasted the northern shore in the employ of certain London merchants. They sent him across the Atlantic with two ships to learn what lay to the north of Virginia. Smith had been grievously wounded by an explosion of gunpowder while returning to Jamestown from one of his exploratory expeditions. He sailed to England in 1609 for medical treatment and never returned to Virginia.

On this new voyage to America he made frequent forays inland and, perhaps struck by reminiscent landscapes, he named the entire area New England. No one knows now what he judged the similarities to his native England. He arrived in the fullness of spring and he may have thought that what later became Massachusetts and Connecticut had in that season some of the softness of agricultural Lincolnshire where he was born. As he went farther north he could have been reminded by New Hampshire's mountains of the Lake District peaks in Cumberland and Westmorland, England's highest. The coast of Maine may have recalled Yorkshire's cliffs, spray-spattered by the North Sea. But New England it was and, following the map he drew, it was so entered on the cartographers' charts, the hardy ghost of today's New England.

And what a land it is, this northeast corner of America! It is six states now —Maine, New Hampshire, Vermont, Massachusetts, Rhode Island, and Connecticut. Only four of these were numbered among the thirteen original colonies. Vermont, after boundary disputes with New York were settled in 1791, was admitted to the young republic as the fourteenth state. Maine, which had been incorporated in the Province of Massachusetts Bay since 1691, did not emerge as a separate state until 1820. Then it was split off and admitted as part of the Missouri Compromise by which Missouri came into the union as a slave state and Maine, with slavery outlawed long before, as free.

It used to be said that New England was a state of mind, but that was chiefly back in the days of the astonishing literary flowering which reached its zenith about the middle of the nineteenth century. Then Boston considered itself proudly "the Athens of America," for the writers who flourished there and in nearby Concord, where some of their houses are preserved. Great names lived and are still a lively part of our heritage. To remember just a few who were part of the flourishing writers' circle, there were James Russell Lowell, Ralph Waldo Emerson, Nathaniel Hawthorne, Oliver Wendell Holmes, Henry David Thoreau, Bronson Alcott, Henry Wadsworth Longfellow, and William Hickling Prescott. They were all friends, recognizing and respecting each other's talents, and it must have been a thrilling company when several of them were gathered together. There was, indeed, nothing to rival it outside the Athens of America.

Modern New England has outlived those days but not some of its enjoyments. It still takes pride in the sea. As you drive along the coast on weekends your eyes will find clouds of sail when small craft engage in the Saturday and Sunday racing of the class boats. This reaches its climax at Marblehead's race week in August when the harbor is choked with small catboats, bigger sloops, and schooners. In years when there is a challenge for the America's Cup, Newport, Rhode Island, is the focus as a foreign yacht meets the American defender in a series of races off Block Island. Since the schooner *America* won its fifty-three-mile race around the Isle of Wight in 1851 and brought home the cup offered by the Royal Yacht Squadron, there have been twenty-one challenges from which the American defender has always emerged victorious. There is a charming story told about the end of the first race in 1851, which the *America* won by a fantastic margin. Queen Victoria was on her own yacht at Cowes when she was informed by a member of her suite that the *America* had finished first. "Who is second?" she asked. "There is no second, Ma'am," was the sadly eloquent reply.

There is more than sailing to New England, of course. It is a joy to hit a tee shot on one of the golf courses of New Hampshire or Vermont with the glory of the mountain scenery around you. There are resolute hikers and mountain climbers who pack rucksacks and pace the Appalachian Trail or hack their way up Mt. Washington. You will find you can do this journey more easily on the cog railway, and there you will be at the top of New England with a gale blowing around you as you take in the magnificent view. These are sights that will stay in your memory.

II

THOUGH THE landscape of New England presents the sharpest of contrasts, from gentle meadow and forest land to the rugged 5000-foot peaks of the Presidential Range in New Hampshire there is a kind of homogeneity about the whole that is a matter of the spirit rather than of the land itself. If you love New England some inner sense will tell you when you are *there*. The similarity defies description but it exists, as New Englanders will proudly tell you. John Adams wrote in his *Diary* when he attended the first Continental Congress in September, 1774, "Philadelphia is not Boston," and proceeded to explain the differences. And no other place is quite like New England.

Of course there are great cities now, and American cities, wherever they lie across the continent, have mostly lost their regional individuality, particularly in the last quarter century. They all tend to look like—well, cities. It is in the towns and villages and their surrounding lands that the flavor of New England lingers. For one thing, these places have not lost their ties with antiquity. In old towns like Ipswich and Salem in Massachusetts, Portsmouth, New Hampshire, and Wiscasset, Maine, fine houses tell of the good lives lived there since the eighteenth and early nineteenth centuries, when merchants could make fortunes from the tall ships returning from the Orient with rich cargoes that left their owners independent for life.

Habits of speech remain, too, blurred in the cities and among newer arrivals, but still true of the descendants of older families. The New England "a" is sharp and grows sharper the farther north you go. It is most pronounced in Maine where, by the way, you will hear natives call it "the State of Maine." Bar Harbor on Mount Desert Island, with the accent of Desert on the second syllable, when a local speaks is "Ba'ha'ba," with the "a's" flat and short, the "r's" nonexistent. Another idiosyncrasy you will find is the pronunciation of such place names as Kennebunkport, Hyannis Port and Newburyport. These names occur frequently and only along the coast, of course, for they simply mean that Kennebunkport is the port of Kennebunk, a short distance inland, Hyannis Port of Hyannis, and Newburyport of the village of Old Newbury. But the proper accent is invariably on the last syllable—"port"—with the rest of the word unstressed.

A similar peculiarity occurs with the word "selectmen," the individuals in authority where the form of local government is the town meeting. Originally this was the way all New England towns were administered and in many it still remains. It is democracy in its purest form since every local citizen has a right to attend town meeting, speak up if he wishes and vote. Often you will find a sign on the outskirts of a town posting the speed limit and below it "By order of the Selectmen." The accent is on the last syllable in New England, a pronunciation that I find descriptive and agreeable. If you are lucky, you may hear an older version—"see-lect-men," with the accent on all three syllables, though stronger on the last. But I am sure the speaker would have to be an ancient.

Another strangeness of language that the new traveler in Massachusetts must accept is that one goes "down east" or "down to Maine." Now Maine, as anyone can see from the map, is east, but it is "up" from Boston. The special idiom is a holdover from the days of sailing ships, for any ship from Boston sailed down wind to Maine in the prevailing southwest breeze which blows along the New England coast. In the old days so much of the colony depended on the sea that this designation was adopted by landsmen and seamen alike.

10

The phrase is used today by skippers of pleasure yachts who cruise down to Maine in summer. It is an almost hallowed usage. No New Englander worth his salt-water ancestors would ever say that he was going "up to Maine," even though the trip was to be made by car on the Maine Turnpike. He still speaks of places there as "down in Maine."

New England speech is filled with regional idioms which would take the visitor a long time to absorb. They are quite clear to the natives. A famous example is the flash that came over the news wires on the afternoon of August 2, 1927 when Calvin Coolidge announced, "I do not choose to run for President in 1928." He had called a news conference in Rapid City, South Dakota, where his summer White House was set up, and passed out slips of paper with this unadorned sentence. He refused to explain or amplify. Immediately the correspondents and pundits were in a frenzy of speculation. What did the President mean? Was he simply expressing a preference for retiring? Would he be open to a draft by the 1928 Republican convention? The tight-lipped Coolidge—a New Englander's New Englander—refused to say. Fellow New Englanders knew. Used in that way, "choose" meant an irrevocable personal decision not to run. Coolidge might have said, "Under no circumstances will I be a candidate for reelection in 1928." But that wouldn't have been New England speech.

Today New England is a land for all seasons. Your preference would depend on your interests, always remembering that spring comes a bit late and later in the northern states. If you like to revel in the past and visit old houses bear in mind that many—though not all—are closed in early autumn and not reopened until spring is well advanced. For a good many years there has been a drive to save the old houses from demolition. A publication of the Society for the Preservation of New England Antiquities lists two hundred or more houses, taverns, churches, and other historic buildings which have been restored, furnished with suitable period pieces, and are open to the public. There are also many regional museums with memorable collections from colonial days.

All the New England states have their relics, and a surprising number date from the seventeenth century. How careless men used to be of our past! In the city of Boston there is but a single straggler from the seventeenth century, the house on North Square where Paul Revere lived and worked. Many of the old frame houses were destroyed in the frequent holocausts before modern fire-fighting equipment was available. In Boston alone, between 1653 and 1760 there were ten major fires which wiped out whole sections of the town. The great fire of 1711 burned the old wooden Town House, the seat of government. It was replaced by a handsome brick structure in the Early Georgian style which is one of Boston's landmarks still and known as the Old State House. But other early structures were torn down simply in the name of progress. Most of the old buildings that remain are in villages and towns which have not changed a great deal over the years.

Of course there is much more than history to New England, though your appreciation of the region will be immeasurably heightened when you have soaked yourself in the past. If golf or fishing and hunting are your interest they are there in abundance. New England has some of the finest fresh-water lakes and streams in the United States, well stocked with fish, plus the salt-water species which are an off-shore lure from spring to late autumn and from Rhode Island to Maine. State parks provide a variety of camping sites in which it is easy to imagine you are surrounded by virgin wilderness—except for the welcome conveniences.

In autumn, beginning with September, the trees flame with unbelievable colors as frost bites and leaves turn to a shower of red and gold. The full glory does not last for long and can be deadened with a heavy rain accompanied by strong winds. I have driven many years through northern Massachusetts, Vermont, New Hampshire, and Maine to enjoy the fantastic riot of color. A date close to Columbus Day finds it at the height of its beauty. There is nothing to equal this anywhere in our country unless it is in the Adirondacks next door. And nowhere else in the world will you find such a display.

Winter used to be a time when rural New England hibernated, but the skiing excitement and snow tires have changed all that. You won't drive many miles in winter before you come upon glistening slopes with tows and chair lifts to take you to the top, comfortable coffee shops to warm you when you come down, and overnight facilities nearby. Skiing has changed the whole landscape in the past twenty years and quite truly made New England a year-round vacationland.

This is superb motoring country with broad expressways and turnpikes to cut the time from here to there if you must, but also a net of excellent by-way roads which will take you more pleasantly through the old towns. Except for the fine road you are traveling you can almost imagine what it was like when the pioneers began to move back from the seaboard to clear the land and set up farms. That was well over three hundred years ago, for a few of the houses still standing go back to the 1630s. And it is nearly five centuries since the country was discovered, if you count back to the English ships that looked with wonder at our virgin shores.

III

THE FIRST to sight North America was the *Matthew*, which sailed from Bristol in May, 1497, under command of John Cabot, a Genoan by birth, a Venetian by adoption, who came to England and found favor with Henry VII for his prowess as a navigator. Cabot chose a northern route across the Atlantic, shorter by far than the course Columbus had taken five years before. The details of his voyage are murky, but it is probable that he came ashore on either Newfoundland, Cape Breton Island, or Labrador. Wherever it was, he claimed the land for the first Tudor monarch and, as a sentimental gesture, planted the flag of Venice beside the standard of England's king.

The following year John Cabot made a second voyage. He tried to cross even farther north, and ice forced him to turn south. These voyages, and others over the next decades, were undertaken with no thought of planting colonies. They were purely exploratory. The king and the London and Bristol merchants who put up the money had hope that the voyagers might find riches on this far and unknown shore. What they hoped more was that the mariners might discover a northwest passage through the land mass, which would lead to the Indies and shortcut the lengthy route around Africa's tip.

For nearly three hundred years this was a goal that drove successive explorers along the coast of North America, entering rivers and straits and inlets in the hope that somewhere the passage would be found. Of course Cabot, no more than the others, hit upon the legendary and mythical waterway, nor did he bring back riches. The most he discovered was the wealth of cod and other fish in the northern waters, which would later attract British fishing fleets to the Grand Banks. Still searching for a route to the Orient, Cabot coasted down as far as Chesapeake Bay and then set his sails for home and Bristol.

In the first half of the sixteenth century there were other English voyagers and, like Cabot, they were searching for wealth and a northwest passage. Tales of the fabulous riches in gold and silver the Spaniards had found in Central and South America gave hope that some of these mariners would come upon veins of precious metal in the northern latitudes. Quite possibly the disappointing cargoes the ships brought home damped the enthusiasm of the merchants for the expensive outfitting of other ships to engage in futile treasure hunts. And the years were still ahead when ranging Britons boldly scoured the seas, pirating, plundering and, from captured Spanish and Portuguese ships, actually bringing home the treasure the early English adventurers had hoped for and never found in the land.

In the great age of Elizabeth this new urge expanded with the feats of Sir Francis Drake and Sir John Hawkins. Neither man was a colonizer. Their chief purpose was to raid Spanish settlements when they were lightly guarded and to take foreign prizes wherever they found them. Drake, after daring the Strait of Magellan, sailed up the west coast possibly as far as today's San Francisco to search for a western exit of the northwest passage which he might probe in reverse to find the eastern entrance.

It was not until 1587 that Sir Walter Raleigh planted the ill-starred first English colony on Roanoke Island just off the coast of North Carolina. After its tragic and still unfathomed blackout, it was two decades before other colonies were considered. Still, a fever was growing in England. Bartholomew Gosnold captained a ship to the New World in 1602. He reached Maine, named Cape Cod because the waters there were boiling with codfish, discovered the islands of Nantucket and Martha's Vineyard, and came ashore on Cuttyhunk, which he named Elizabeth Island in honor of his queen. Today the entire short string of islands leading out from Woods Hole in Massachusetts is called the Elizabeth Islands with the outermost, Cuttyhunk, a famous sport-fishing center for striped bass, with marlin and swordfish more chancy game farther off shore. Cuttyhunk's single small town is named Gosnold in honor of its first visitor. Gosnold returned to England and, because of his experience, was appointed captain of one of the three ships that brought out the Virginia colonists in 1607 to establish the first permanent English settlement in the New World.

Farther north in Maine there were two or three abortive attempts at settlement. When Captain John Smith returned to England from Jamestown in 1609 and regained his health he was enthusiastic about the prospects of colonization in America and set about finding backers for a survey to be made north of the Virginia colony. During his Jamestown service he had led several exploring parties through the region, using the rivers for inland transport to scan bordering land. His most ambitious project carried him along both shores of Chesapeake Bay and its tributary rivers. He scouted the Potomac as far as the present site of Washington. The map he brought back of these expeditions and his persuasive talk convinced a group of London merchants that fitting out two ships might be a fair gamble. Smith set out in March, 1614, and did a thorough job of his exploration. His map of the coast from the Penobscot River to Cape Cod was surprisingly accurate, and he gave the name of Plymouth to the mainland opposite the Cape. The cargo of fish and furs, traded from the Indians, that he brought back must have convinced his sponsors that there were riches other than gold for investors in America. Still, they were reluctant to try a second time.

Back in London Smith made the acquaintance of an Englishman with the improbable name of Sir Ferdinando Gorges, who shared Smith's enthusiasm for establishing settlements in North America. Sir Ferdinando had already sent out one colony, in 1607, whose members built a fort at the mouth of the lower Kennebec River in Maine but abandoned it the following year and came home. He now engaged Smith to pilot another group to establish a settlement in Maine.

Smith set out in 1615, but the angry North Atlantic was too much for his small vessels, and he was forced to return to Bristol. On a second try the same year Smith was captured by pirates, another hazard of the sea. Never discouraged, he made his way back to London and, in 1617, set out on a third voyage. But this, like the first, was frustrated by weather and he put back into Bristol harbor. It seemed that the luck of the hardy adventurer had run out.

This ended his attempts to set up colonies in the New World. For the rest of his life—he died in 1631—he engaged in writing books and pamphlets, drawing maps, which together told the story of Virginia and left a record of his life and accomplishments. Though Sir Ferdinando never came to our far shore he continued his interest in Maine. In 1639 he obtained a royal charter and set up a provincial government which, however, did not prosper.

It was farther south in Massachusetts where New England began to assume stature with the arrival of the Pilgrims at Plymouth in 1620. Their struggle to gain a foothold on the bleak, wintry shore, their pious determination, and their victory are the stuff of many books, starting with the contemporary account by William Bradford, the second governor, in his history, *Of Plimouth Plantation*. News of their success inspired other colonial ventures, which came quickly now. Roger Conant and the Dorchester Company established a settlement on Cape Ann with fishing and agriculture designed to provide a viable economy. The settlers came in 1624 but they soon lost heart for the rugged life of pioneers. Most returned to England, and two years later Conant led the rest to what is now Salem. Another company under John Endecott came out in 1628, and Endecott assumed the governorship of the Salem colony.

In 1629 the most ambitious of the English colonization schemes was set up when London merchants and other promoters formed a company to establish the Province of Massachusetts Bay. A generous charter was obtained from Charles I, and John Winthrop was appointed governor. In the spring of 1630 a fleet of ships bearing seven hundred colonists dropped anchor near Salem. After a certain amount of scouting the leaders decided to plant their colony on a small peninsula surrounded by the waters of Massachusetts Bay. Later, after the settlement was established, the designation would change to Boston Bay and then to Boston harbor, for the colonists had early decided to give the name of Boston to their "citty on a hill," as John Winthrop, borrowing the phrase from St. Matthew, spoke of it poetically in a sermon during the crossing of the *Arbella*. The choice was in honor of the county town in Lincolnshire whose minister, John Cotton, had delivered the farewell sermon to the emigrants. In 1633 Cotton himself joined them in America.

The selection of the peninsula was by no means unanimously approved. Some felt the area was too small for the growth of the settlement they envisioned; some protested because it was open to seaborne attacks and could not be protected from raiding parties of French or Spanish marauders. Others thought its isolation was an objection. Its only connection was a narrow neck that touched the mainland near what was to become Roxbury. As a result of the disputes, parties of settlers from the main body separated and established villages in the vicinity.

Most Americans do not realize how quickly the land was settled once the Massachusetts Bay company arrived. I have in my possession two folio sheets from an atlas published in England in 1636. A map of the North American coast appears on one side of the sheets; on the reverse is a description of the new colony. Some of the towns it lists, in addition to Boston, as being already established are Mount Wollaston, part of today's Quincy, where Henry Adams brought his considerable family of eight sons from Somerset in 1638 to establish the Adams tribe in the New World; Dorchester, Roxbury ("a fair and handsome country town, the inhabitants being all very rich"), Charlestown, Medford, Newtown (which was soon renamed Cambridge), Watertown, Saugus, Nahant, and, of course, Plymouth and Salem.

The description makes Massachusetts seem an ideal place to settle. Game is plentiful—deer, bear, moose, rabbits, wild turkeys, pigeons, woodcock, partridges—not many pheasants. Vegetables, herbs, and fruits grow wild, with strawberries "about two inches across," an optimistic girth for wild strawberries anywhere. In addition there are gooseberries, blackberries, and raspberries. The Indians are friendly, the writer testifies, and quickly came to accept the God of the Englishmen because the seasons had been so much more gentle since the settlers arrived. In view of the savage Indian attacks soon to come this

16

judgment seems open to question. Probably the writer was reflecting the pious estimates of the Puritans.

Our atlas reporter says there were between five and six thousand settlers in the province by 1636. Two thousand men bore arms, "well provided with ordnance and munition." The settlement was firmly established and going ahead fast. The colonists had "bred great store of cattle," pigs, and other animals and were already exporting produce to England. A self-supporting community had been created within six years of the founding of the Massachusetts Bay company.

Emigration from England was flourishing. Between 1620 and 1642 it is estimated that 20,000 English and their families came to the New World. Though the tradition is that they came for the freedom of worship they could not find at home, this was only part of the reason. There was a depression on in Britain, caused by the Thirty Years War, which had further depressed the wool industry in East Anglia and almost stopped commerce with Europe. England was not involved militarily but all Europe was, in a succession of small bloody campaigns.

There was also nervous trouble at home in the civil war between Charles I and Oliver Cromwell's Roundheads. In the confusing turbulence men thought the prospects of a more promising livelihood might be found in the overseas colonies. By 1642, though the small king would reign for seven more years before that cold January morning in 1649 when he was beheaded on a platform outside Whitehall Palace, is seemed apparent that he would be defeated. If that happened disturbed Englishmen thought that at least the persecution of dissenters would end.

IV

IN SPITE of those who set up villages on the surrounding mainland, Boston indeed became the seat of the province. The First Church was set up in King Street, the center of the town, with a host of taverns soon opened nearby. One of the first steps was to establish the provincial government, composed of the governor and his councilors. A few years later an assembly, elected by the people, was added, making a bicameral legislature with the council as the upper house, and this was the pattern of government until the royal authority ceased with the Declaration of Independence. When the province was granted a new charter by

William and Mary in 1691, the legislature was given the pontifical name of the Great and General Court. It persists today as the official designation. Behind the State House you will see signs protecting streetside parking spaces: "Reserved for Members of the General Court."

It is impossible today to pick out colonial Boston. The "small peninsula" has been so spectacularly enlarged that now the city is a solid part of the mainland. The transformation began just before the beginning of the nineteenth century when the three hills known as Trimontaine had their tops shaved off. Now there is only the single slope of the middle eminence—Beacon Hill, though reduced in height by sixty feet. The earth and rocks went to fill in the coves and indentations of the harbor shoreline, which had become a jagged fretwork of wharves. Some of the fill also went to widen Boston Neck, still at that time the only land exit.

In the 1850s an even greater reclamation project was launched—to fill in the brackish Back Bay and create a new piece of residential land to the west. There in time grew Newbury and Marlborough streets, Commonwealth Avenue, and an extension of Beacon Street which offered attractive sites for fine houses. Other land was annexed to Boston, and at last even Castle William, the island fortress in colonial times, was attached to the town. There is no longer any indication of the outlines of the original Boston. You simply cannot find it.

There are survivals, to be sure, that were standing in the turbulent years leading to the Revolution—the Old South Meeting House, the Old North Church, the Old State House, Paul Revere's house, King's Chapel with its ancient tombstones, the Old Granary Burying Ground on the other side of Tremont Street, where so many of the great patriots were laid to rest. The classic new State House, designed by Charles Bulfinch, its cornerstone laid by Governor Samuel Adams in 1795, crowns Beacon Hill, and down the slope are some of Boston's finest houses, though these were mostly built in the first quarter of the nineteenth century. Many were inspired by Britain's new Regency style with bow windows, and in some you will see a Boston phenomenon—lavender-tinted glass. This did not come about by design. Glass for the windows, imported from England, turned out to be partially defective. As it aged some of the panes took on the lavender hue. Instead of being replaced they were preserved as a peculiar mark of Bostonian distinction.

Behind Beacon Street lie Chestnut and Mount Vernon, also sweeping down the hill. Together these three streets made a triptych of elegance through the Federal period and past the middle of the century until the residential land of the Back Bay attracted newer fortunes made from the steam-powered looms opened up in the Industrial Revolution, which changed New England from a seafaring and agricultural economy to one of manufacture as well.

While Massachusetts was developing as the most important colony in New England, others were being established. The rigid theocracy that governed the Bay province was directly responsible for two—Connecticut and Rhode Island. Life in Boston and Salem was grim in those days for anyone not dedicated to the rigid doctrines of the church. Instead of welcoming all settlers to share in the joys of what was sometimes called "the new Canaan," church membership was required for a man to vote at town meeting, and the civil magistrates decided arbitrarily who should be admitted. Any departure from the approved dogmas was cause for him to be kept outside the sheltering arms.

In 1635 a party from Watertown, Dorchester, and Newtown, led by a more mellow divine, the Reverend Thomas Hooker, settled in what is now Hartford. Two years later, a party of English Puritans who had spent a year in Massachusetts Bay, were likewise disenchanted by the strict religious government and moved out to found New Haven. In the next few years a number of quite separate settlements were made in Connecticut, and all were brought together in 1665 under a single charter.

In 1636 the ideas of Roger Williams, a minister and outspoken democratic church liberal, outraged the religious autocracy. He was banished from the colony. He went in winter to what is now Rhode Island and, in the wilderness, set up a colony at what is today's Providence. Williams was very much of an intellectual, a graduate of Cambridge University in England, but he could not stomach the single righteousness of Massachusetts Bay. In his new colony men of all beliefs were welcome, except Roman Catholics. Since there were none in New England at the time, this exception hardly mattered. His colony was soon a lively place, thriving on trade and controversy, the number of fresh arrivals indicating that by no means all Puritans were happy in the new Canaan. In 1645 Williams obtained a charter for Rhode Island which continued after his death as a refuge for religious freedom.

The first settlement in New Hampshire was set up in 1653 on the short sea coast—it is only eighteen miles in length—and soon pioneers moved inland where towns were established. Though there were frequent disputes with New York and Massachusetts over the parceling out of land in the new colony, these were peaceably settled a century later. One important contribution New Hampshire was to make in the founding of the new nation: In June, 1788, it became the ninth state to ratify the Federal Constitution and thereby put the instrument in force.

Maine began to be occupied in the early 1630s, and a number of new towns were established including Falmouth, which was the original name of Portland. Agriculture and off-shore fishing were the principal concern of the settlers, with lobstering in the shallow water along the coast becoming a lucrative part of the economy, as it still is. The visitor to Maine will find broiled live lobster a staple on any restaurant menu, a delicacy in which the state takes proper pride. If you have never attacked a whole lobster, some instruction in the mystique is useful to master the dissection. It is a quite messy business, so that most restaurants supply kingsize bibs for the process. But the gustatory satisfaction is worth every bit of the effort.

Vermont's original exploration was made by Samuel de Champlain in 1609, and the area was sparsely peopled by the French. The first English settlement did not come until 1724 when Fort Dummer was built on the Connecticut River just north of the Massachusetts border to protect the town of Deerfield, which had suffered from bloody Indian massacres since 1675. The most devastating occurred in 1704 when the French joined with their Indian allies to murder the peaceful villagers. Today Old Deerfield is a museum town with its handsome early eighteenth-century houses, some of them open to the public. But whether you enter one or not, a slow drive down the principal street to peer at the venerable exteriors is an experience to treasure.

During the French and Indian War the French built Fort Carillon on the west shore of Lake Champlain toward the connection with Lake George on the south. Before that war's end the British had captured it and changed the name to Ticonderoga. In the spring of 1775, remembering its armament of cannon and mortars, the Americans determined to take the fort. They were desperately short of artillery. In the night of May 9–10 Ethan Allen led a detachment of his Green Mountain Boys. He was accompanied by Benedict Arnold, who laid a claim to command the expedition, but the men were loyal to Allen. The party reached the gates about three o'clock in the morning, two sentries were overpowered, and the Americans were inside the fort.

The attack achieved complete surprise. It might better be said that it achieved complete astonishment, since quite possibly Captain William Delaplace, who commanded, had not learned of the engagement of the British and provincials on April 19 and did not know that a virtual state of war existed in Massachusetts. In any case, when Ethan Allen pounded on the door of his

20

sleeping quarters and demanded his surrender the British officer came out in night dress, carrying his breeches, as Allen testified. Delaplace asked in whose name the surrender was demanded at which Allen is said to have thundered, "In the name of the great Jehovah and the Continental Congress!" This impressive dual authority would have been enough to startle any commander into surrender, particularly when he saw how outnumbered his small garrison was by the Americans. It seems improbable that Delaplace had ever heard of the Continental Congress.

For a long time after the surrender Vermont lore built up far more earthy phrases for Ethan Allen's surrender demand than the words historians have embalmed. When I was in college my professor, Claude H. Van Tyne, a distinguished authority on American history, maintained that what Allen really said outside Delaplace's door was "Come out of there, you damned rat!" But Dr. Van Tyne, a salty character himself, probably had no more authority than Vermont legend.

Fort Ticonderoga, by the way, has been beautifully restored and is a fascinating museum today. It is a short way across the Vermont border from New York state and well worth the journey. I know of no other restoration which evokes our military past so sharply. There it stands, a fine example of eighteenth-century engineering, its cannon commanding the lakeward approaches.

By 1775 when Ticonderoga was taken, all of New England had been colonized. Not densely, of course—there were long distances between many of the towns, which were mostly villages in themselves. There was no real intercourse between the colonies at this time. No mutual problems required it, and the roads, except in summer, were atrocious. The settlers were all British Americans but they had no sense of communion with each other. Nothing drew them together until 1765, when the assault on their pocketbooks with the Stamp Act and the fact that Parliament had dared to levy a direct tax put them into active revolt. When the act was repealed the following spring they drifted apart again. It was only with the passage of the act closing the port of Boston in May, 1774, and the call for the First Continental Congress the following September that they were aroused into a state of common interest. The fate of Massachusetts became the cause of all the colonies, and on this ground they were united.

As the delegates to the Congress from Massachusetts began their journey by coach toward Philadelphia they were greeted everywhere as heroes. They were entertained with banquets in every town through which they passed. In

Connecticut and New York they met for the first time men whose names had been known only through correspondence, and this continued through New Jersey and on to Philadelphia. It was a triumphal progress. More, it was an index of the unity which had at last cemented the colonies in a determination to resist the actions of the British Parliament whenever they violated the charters. The leaders were by no means yet decided on independence. In fact, the possibility was hardly mentioned during that first Congress. Nevertheless, the united colonies had taken a first step toward their inevitable destiny.

V

IT IS WORTH going back to spend a bit more time with Boston, because here, rather than in the other New England colonies, the fiery revolt against the British Parliament reached its peak in the 1760s and 1770s. In case you have forgotten your history—or perhaps never quite knew it—the cause of the final quarrel can be quickly summed up. For more than a century after the colonies were planted England paid little attention to them. Britain had laws to govern their trade with the foreign West Indian Islands and with the European nations. Beyond that, its policy was one of "salutary neglect." The British government followed a mercantilist point of view of the relationship. The American colonies were required to send their raw materials to Britain, where they were turned into manufactured goods and sent back for sale. It was a quite satisfactory arrangement in general. To be sure there were customs laws, but the American merchants early proved to be accomplished smugglers with no sense of guilt attaching to this deliberate evasion by even the most respected citizens. It always cost England more to staff its customs service in America than it obtained in revenue.

The great change that began the eruption against England occurred only after the end of the French and Indian War in 1763. It had been a costly war for England. Although the Americans contributed liberally in money and engaged heavily in the campaigns against the French, the English government decided that the Americans should bear a part of the expense through taxes and passed the Stamp Act in 1765. That did it. While the British Americans, as they called themselves, were willing to accept customs duties, whether they paid them or not, they were dead set against paying direct taxes to the British government and they never did.

They were on quite legal ground. Their charters gave them the explicit right to raise their own taxes with no implication that any of the money should go home to England. That was the single basis of the quarrel. Though I believe the erroneous impression has grown up that the Americans wanted independence during the early years, this is disproved by the evidence. From the first meeting of all the colonies in September, 1774, it was only with the greatest reluctance that the delegates declared for independence in July, 1776, after sending futile petitions to the King protesting their loyalty.

This is no place to detail the whole of the events from 1765 to 1776. The Stamp Act aroused violent riots in Boston, as elsewhere, and the town was in turmoil. The colonists flatly refused to use the stamped papers decreed by the act, and they were impounded in Castle William. All business and all legal activities ceased for some time, though they gradually resumed, ignoring the stamps. In the spring of 1766 the act was repealed by Parliament, though another act was passed which asserted that Parliament has the *right* to tax the colonies.

In 1767, Charles Townshend, the new Chancellor of the Exchequer, shepherded a bill through Parliament to lay a tax on the colonies for the import of paper, lead, glass, paint, and tea. Once more Massachusetts rebelled and an agreement among the merchants was reached against handling any of these items. Rioting occurred again, and in October, 1768, the British sent two regiments down from Halifax to curb the mobbish Bostonians. Though the town was fairly quiet at first during the occupation the Americans did not hesitate to voice their resentment. On the evening of March 5, 1770, a mob began badgering a single sentinel in front of the custom house till he called for the main guard. A platoon of British soldiers joined him and, in response to the taunts and buffeting of the mob, shots were fired; five Bostonians were killed. Next day a great town meeting was held in the Old South Meeting House. Demands were made on the Lieutenant Governor that the troops be sent to the barracks on Castle William. Reluctantly the official consented, and the hated redcoats were gone.

Now a period of quiet settled over Boston. The Townshend Acts were repealed except for the tax on tea which Parliament kept as a token indication of its right to tax the colonies, although the Americans refused to purchase the tea and it was not shipped. In the autumn of 1773, however, the British determined to export large quantities of tea to each of the colonies. Massachusetts and the others refused to pay the customs duty on the cargoes, and the famous

Boston Tea Party took place on the night of December 16. An orderly mob, rather poorly disguised as Indians, descended on the ships, winched up the chests of tea and poured their contents into the harbor.

The following June 1 the port was closed in reprisal; General Thomas Gage appeared as military governor with seven regiments at his back. Now the provincial legislature determined to beef up the militia and create companies of Minute Men. Stockpiles of powder, ball, and food products were gathered in Concord. Gage decided that these stores must be secured, and on the night of April 18, 1775, he dispatched a force numbering around eight hundred men to seize them. The exercise was planned as a surprise marchout from which the troops would be back by early morning. It was anything but a surprise. The Americans had word of the sortie, and two night riders, Paul Revere and William Dawes, carried the alarm to the countryside, alerting the farmers and the militia. When the regulars reached Lexington they found a company drawn up on the Green. The nervous British—without an order from their commander—fired three volleys, killing eight Americans and wounding ten more. These were the first musket shots of the Revolution, though it would be fifteen months before independence was declared.

The British marched on to Concord and vainly searched for the now hidden military stores. The soldiers in the town were quite correct in their attitude toward the civilians, but hostilities broke out at the North Bridge, where a detail had been sent to guard this crossing of the Concord River. The Americans were some distance away on the opposite side, massing on a hill and watching what the soldiers might do. When they tried to take up the planks of the bridge the provincials held back no longer. A sharp fire fight ensued with the Americans killing or wounding a number of the soldiers and taking casualties of their own.

When you are in Boston it is not far to Lexington where you will see the Green, not much changed from what it was that dawn of April 19 with a sharp easterly breeze stirring the young leaves. Then you may drive on "the battle road" the few miles to Concord (pronounced "Concud," by the way, in New England). You will find "the rude bridge," restored now, where the attack took place. It is a stirring experience, I can tell you. It makes the sap swell in your chest, not because you dislike the redcoats at this far distance in time—after all, they were professional soldiers obeying orders—but because you like the Americans in an hour of momentous history when farmers and farmers' sons challenged the might of the most powerful nation in the world.

After the engagement at North Bridge the British retired into the town, the Americans following to take cover on a hill. Shortly after noon Colonel Smith, the British commander, ordered a return to Boston. The Americans again followed along the high ground and, at Meriam's Corner, where the road turns east toward Lexington, they began to fire on the column. There was no order. It was a spontaneous attack by individuals, spurred by the built up resentment against the British troops. It was guerrilla warfare as the British marched toward Boston, with the Americans popping up from behind stone walls and trees to fire a shot into the massed column and disappear. The return became a disastrous rout until the exhausted soldiers met the relief party sent out under Earl Percy at Lexington. After a short rest they proceeded in better order, though still under constant fire, to find the boats in Charlestown that would ferry the survivors to Boston.

The Americans did not disperse after their victory. Instead they climbed high ground and invested the town of Boston. As other militia companies came in from more distant places a headquarters was set up in Cambridge where the first bridge over the Charles River stood. Now the Americans proceeded to beleaguer Boston. Militiamen were strung out in a great semicircle beginning at Charlestown and extending around the Back Bay through Cambridge to Dorchester Heights. The British made no attempt for two months to emerge and engage them.

They were forced to do so at the Battle of Bunker Hill on June 17, 1775. It has always been called that, though the battle was actually fought over a redoubt that the colonials built in the night of June 16 on Breed's Hill, closer to Boston. The redoubt was revealed in first light the following morning when a lookout on *H.M.S. Lively* reported the new fortification. The redoubt was shelled by the ships without much effect, while the generals in Boston talked out what to do. They must attack, but the tide was wrong that morning, and it was afternoon before they could move ships inshore and land troops for a drive up Breed's Hill.

The assault began about two p.m. when British regulars under General Sir William Howe made the first ascent. They were driven back by murderous fire from the redoubt. You remember the order of Colonel William Prescott, "Don't fire until you see the whites of their eyes." This has often been quoted as an inspired command by Prescott but it was a well-known caution when skittish soldiers might fire their guns too early to be effective. The smooth-bore musket was anything but accurate, and a bullet would not carry more than sixty yards with any chance to killing. The flintlock had a front sight but none at the rear of the barrel, so it was impossible to line up a shot as you might a rifle today. To wait until the defending soldiers saw the whites of their attackers' eyes would inflict the maximum of carnage. This happened that fateful afternoon. The British made two assaults on the redoubt and reeled back from the massed fire. Then General Howe ordered them to drop their heavy packs and make a bayonet charge up the hill. By now the provincials were running out of powder. The British gained the fort, routed the Americans, and at last won the day.

It was a pyrrhic victory. Out of the British force of 2,450, 1,024 were casualties. A great number of the dead were officers. The colonial losses were but a tenth of these, mostly suffered when the regulars overran the redoubt. The British did not pursue their advantage but retired into Boston, now an almost entirely Tory town. The patriots had one desire—to drive them out. They had a plan. During the cruel winter—it was as bitterly cold as the previous one had been mild—General Henry Knox and his men dragged forty-three cannon and sixteen mortars from Fort Ticonderoga by sledge through the frozen forests. At last, in early March, the artillery was positioned as a battery on Dorchester Heights commanding the British troop ships and men-of-war. General Howe had succeeded General Gage as military governor, and there was only one move now that he could make. If he tried to assault the Heights in an amphibious landing his troops would be massacred in their boats. If he stayed in the harbor his entire fleet would be annihilated by the emplaced artillery. On March 17, 1776, the regulars boarded their ships and sailed out of Boston, never to return.

After that there was little fighting in New England. The war moved to New York and Long Island, to New Jersey and Pennsylvania, and then south through Virginia, the Carolinas, and Georgia till it ended with the surrender of Lord Cornwallis' main force at Yorktown on October 19, 1781. When Cornwallis' troops were paraded to lay down their arms their music played—by the choice of some antic British bandmaster—a popular English light air, *The World Turned Upside Down!*

VI

WELL, THAT WAS the way New England began, grew as a group of prosperous British colonies, and reluctantly decided to separate from the Mother Country and take its place as part of the new nation. It was two centuries ago, yet when you stand on the wide boards of an elegant Georgian living room and look at the glowing walnut and mahogany of the period pieces, you may feel it was only yesterday. You can almost touch fingers with the ancestors on the wall. There were handsome men and lovely women who peopled the colonies before the break. John Singleton Copley, the Boston painter who sailed in 1774 to take up residence in England, has done most to make them live for us. You will see his portraits in many museums throughout New England. One thing to notice is the proud heads of the women. They are patrician and with such a characteristic face and expression that they show how strong was the English strain. Lovely they were in their graceful young womanhood, ancestors to admire and to cherish.

Tourism has become big business in all the six states. If I were considering a trip I would write to each capital, telling what I wanted to see and do and in what season, asking for all their publications that would cover my interests. Each state calls its information bureau by a different name, but I am sure if you wrote, for example, State of Maine, Augusta, Maine, and added "Tourist Services" you would be sent what you need to lay out a memorable itinerary for the time you have available. Even though you have never touched down in New England before, with the maps and folders you can work out a trip that seems most inviting to your taste.

Though New England is small compared to the great spaces of our West, it is still a big country once you begin driving it. The thing that cuts your daily mileage is the number of stops you make to enjoy points of particular interest. In planning many motor trips both in this country and abroad, I have found that careful advance map study pays off in satisfaction since it takes the aimlessness out of motoring. I decide first with my family where we would like to go, add up the overall mileage, and then begin to figure intermediate distances and pick convenient over-night destinations, taking note of desired stops and subtracting probable sightseeing hours from the day's run. While you will hardly stick rigidly to the schedule, this sort of planning provides a constant check on progress. If one day's run has been short of the mark, it can be made up another day, or perhaps some of the overall itinerary can be scrapped. You're out for enjoyment, so if you are going to miss something, what you see instead will undoubtedly be quite as rewarding. And you can always come back again.

Now how should you plan your trip in New England? There is no best way, because it depends on what you would like to do. In the old days, which means before the first World War, when vacations were always a summer-long affair in a fixed location, there was a distinct cleavage between two traditional schools—families who liked the mountains opposed to those who preferred the sea. That was a time when great resort hotels offered elegant hospitality through-out the six states. The mountains meant the Berkshire Hills in Massachusetts, the grander Green Mountains of Vermont and White Mountains of New Hampshire, with a spilling over into Maine. The sea meant almost anywhere along the coast from Connecticut to Maine. Vacations in those more leisurely days were split-family affairs. The motor car was still unreliable, reserved for the adventurous, and journeys were made by train, the open windows sieves of black cinders. The routine was for the wife and children, with a maid or two, to set out for the objective on the Boston & Maine or the New Haven in late June, with the husband taking the same rail transport on occasional weekends and spending a two-week vacation in August. Some of the big country hotels still exist but they are dying out in this motel age, mourned by those who remember their incredibly sumptuous and calorie-rich breakfasts, their Gargantuan luncheons, and many-coursed dinners.

Vacations today—particularly for visitors—are mobile affairs. Few families settle in anywhere for long, and the rest of the time are on the go. This book can give you only general suggestions. If there are sons and daughters approaching college age, New England has some of the finest, and oldest, institutions of higher learning in the country, and most of them are pleasant to see, whether you enter any of the buildings or not. There is a flavor of age about them, beginning with Harvard in Cambridge, oldest in the country, which goes back to 1636, with the buildings of Radcliffe, the women's college, woven among the older ones. The famous Massachusetts Institute of Technology which has contributed so much to the development of our space age, is also in Cam-bridge. Scattered elsewhere in Massachusetts are, among others, Amherst, Williams, and three of the most noted women's colleges, Mount Holyoke, Wellesley, and Smith. To the south in Providence is Brown University. In 1701 Yale University was established in New Haven, Connecticut. Hanover, New Hampshire, has Dartmouth College, whose mellow buildings are a joy to see. In Vermont you will find Middlebury; in Brunswick, Maine, is Bowdoin College, named for James Bowdoin, one of the Boston Revolutionary patriots and Governor of Massachusetts just after independence.

New England is a paradise for bird watchers. Even though you have never followed this hobby you will be disappointed if you do not take a bird book along. Birds are everywhere in abundance, and there is a fascination in learning what they are as you see their plumage flashing among the trees. In the wooded country, in the mountains, you will hear their songs in early morning and at dusk. Along the shore there is a whole new aviary to be identified in the birds that live at the edge of the sea, picking their food from the sand with long, slender bills. And, as you drive along, don't be surprised if you see the silhouette of a great blue heron standing motionless on his stilt legs high above a marsh.

Cape Cod is a marvellous place to see birds, and eastward on the ocean side lies the National Seashore, forty-five miles of protected coast where you may bathe and fish and picnic on public land. Cape Cod is a place you should visit in any case. At Provincetown the Pilgrims first came ashore, and from the landing place parties set out in their shallop to scout the coast for a permanent spot to plant the colony. Provincetown itself is a commercial fishing port, but for the past fifty years it has been an artists' colony, too, crowded now in summer but still worth a visit.

Beyond Provincetown the very tip of the Cape is Race Point, approached on hard-top roads which wind through a waste of sand. This is one of the most favored spots in New England for surf fishing, and if you go there any time from spring to autumn you will see this hardy breed casting for striped bass, and "strip-ed" is pronounced by the initiated in two syllables. There they stand, often in waders, throwing long rods over their shoulders to send lures far out. About a hundred yards is par for a cast, but shorter ones will often produce a strike since the stripers come quite close inshore after bait fish fleeing from their voracious attack. Before spinning gear was perfected after World War II to withstand the corrosive effect of sea water, bait-casting reels were used. Now it is simply a matter of choice.

Surf fishing, which is popular from beaches all along the coast, is marvelous sport. At Race Point, as well as at other spots, you will see the "beach buggies" —often Jeeps—with broad tires to carry them through the sand which would bog down an ordinary car. There will also be trailers and motor campers equipped for sleeping and with an amazing amount of tackle neatly stowed. What makes this kind of fishing so exciting is that striped bass come in jumbo sizes. Thirty pounders are common, but you may hook others that weigh over forty, fifty, and sixty pounds. When one hits your lure the line sings off your reel like an express train. The record fish, taken in August, 1913, from Quick-sett's Hole in the Elizabeth Islands,went seventy-three and a half pounds. In well over fifty-five years this whopper has never been equalled on rod and reel.

If you are a Sunday painter and have packed your gear, New England abounds in irresistible subjects. The most popular, I am sure, are the lighthouses up and down the coast. There must be several million such canvases tucked away in storerooms, for you rarely come upon one of these beacons without seeing an easel set up and an artist at work. Other subjects are endless—tall, wind-sculptured sand dunes with long shadows, an abandoned red barn with its faded paint still remembering more prosperous days, ancient churches on village greens lifting slender spires toward heaven, rugged mountains, their granite facings glittering in the sunlight, a harbor crowded with fishing boats, or a lobsterman's shack hung with the buoys he uses to mark the location of his pots off-shore. Of course all such scenes are there for the color camera, too. With today's magnificent film you can make a record far more complete than anything you have time to put on canvas. This is picturesque and photogenic country at any season.

Your trip need not be expensive. It can be planned in a way to fit almost any pocketbook. Camping is cheapest, of course, provided you have a trailer or motor camper to live aboard or a tent to be pitched in a state park or other public area. Motels and meals are about what they would be anywhere with comparable accommodations, so it should be easy to do the mathematics in advance. If you charter a boat for a day's deep-sea fishing it will be costly, but that is the only unusual expense I can think of. You can go out on a party boat with your family for much less, and the experience is fun. Rods and tackle are included.

Although New England is heavily industrialized, you will be surprised at how little this shows once you are away from the urban complexes of city, suburbs, and factories. The countryside is still quite serene with miles of undisturbed forest land, alive in spring with dogwood, white and pink, followed by laurel and rhododendron and always wildflowers. Wise conservation policies in all the states have set aside thousands of acres for public enjoyment in perpetuity so that the present shape of the land can never really be spoiled. With these safeguards it seems reasonable to prophesy that New England will remain principally rural America, dotted with farms and villages, a blessed refuge from the bustle of great cities, a place to look upon fondly—and enjoy.

30

THE PLATES

Spring

GREENFIELD HILL—CONNECTICUT

Dogwood is the glory of New England's spring, and nowhere is it more lushly displayed than at Greenfield Hill in the town of Fairfield, not far from Bridgeport. Years ago the far-seeing residents planted the trees of white and pink blossoms. They have grown so well that now they arch over the main road in many places. When the dogwoods reach their peak Greenfield is a point of pilgrimage with thousands of visitors wandering through the village to enjoy the luxuriance of another spring. A church fair is held at that time with a fine hot lunch provided for the sightseers.

Nearby are a number of fine old houses and taverns. Here the Reverend Timothy Dwight conducted an academy in the late eighteenth century before being called to Yale College as its president. The houses are of mid-eighteenth-century to early nineteenth-century origin. Across the road from the church is the site of a store torn down in 1925 which, for two hundred years, was the custom house of the Fairfield district. Whenever a ship came into Black Rock harbor, then a part of Fairfield, its skipper had to take the four-mile journey to Greenfield Hill to have his papers put in order.

Not far away is Stratford where the Shakespeare Memorial Theatre has already established a tradition of fine productions of the great bard's plays. It is a pleasant experience to pack a picnic lunch and go there for an afternoon or evening performance. The theater has great architectural charm, and the situation is a fine one at a point where the great Housatonic River opens into Long Island Sound. Before the performance or during an intermission you will see sailboats coming in from blue water on the way to their moorings upstream.

32

LOBSTER COVE—KITTERY POINT, MAINE

This colorful shack shows about all the gear a lobsterman needs to pursue his occupation. The pots, well baited, are sunk in comparatively shallow water, with wooden buoys at the surface to mark each location. The pot is fitted with a funnel-shaped opening through which the lobster enters but cannot get out. Although the canning of lobster is an important industry, most connoisseurs prefer them broiled live and consider them noblemen of the sea.

In the background of the photograph is the William Pepperell house, built in 1682 and still in fine condition. It was the home of the father of Sir William Pepperell, who commanded the colonial troops, chiefly Massachusetts men, at the taking of Louisburg, the French naval base on Cape Breton Island in 1745. For his successful campaign he was awarded a baronetcy and became Sir William Pepperell. He was no soldier by profession but a wealthy merchant.

After his death in 1759 his widow built a fine house in Kittery. The elegant two-story structure is known as the Lady Pepperell House since the widow insisted on using her title until she died, though all such royal honors were canceled by the Revolution. Her house is one of many fine ones in both Kittery and Kittery Point just across the Piscataqua River from New Hampshire.

Stretched across several islands in the river is Portsmouth Navy Yard, established in 1806, where the conference was held that led to acceptance of peace terms at the end of the Russo-Japanese War in 1905. For many years Kittery built ships. The *Ranger* was launched here in 1777 and, under command of John Paul Jones, sailed for France to inform the American commissioners of General Burgoyne's surrender at Saratoga. This news, passed on to the French, resulted almost immediately in recognition of the new republic, as well as a promise to furnish aid to the Americans in their struggle with the British. At Kittery also, in the American Civil War, was built the *Kearsarge*, which ended the depredations of the British-built Confederate raider, *Alabama*, with a decisive battle in the harbor of Cherbourg in which the *Alabama* was sunk.

SALEM TOWNE HOUSE—OLD STURBRIDGE VILLAGE, MASSACHUSETTS

The concept of Old Sturbridge Village belongs to the late Albert B. Wells and his brother, J. Cheney Wells, who in 1936 obtained a charter for an independent, nonprofit, educational institution administered by a board of trustees. Their idea was to create a village of around 1800 with appropriate buildings moved from other New England sites and built into a working whole, with craftsmen displaying the hand industry which existed at that time. More than fifty buildings—houses, shops, mills, barns, tavern, and churches—have been re-assembled on this rural site to recreate our ancestors' way of life.

The Salem Towne House was built in nearby Charlton in 1796 and reconstructed here on the eastern end of the Green between 1952 and 1957. It has fine interiors. The unusual feature of its exterior is a monitor-type roof which allows for many windows to light the upper stories and the attic. The photograph shows the house in the splendor of spring.

Old Sturbridge has been an enormous success since its beginnings. This can be laid to the fact that it is a working community in which old arts and crafts are on display daily with women and men skillfully performing the tasks that kept village economy alive in an older day. The miller, the blacksmith, the weaver, the candle maker, the wood worker are all at their tasks and ready to answer questions from eager viewers.

THE RUDE BRIDGE—CONCORD, MASSACHUSETTS

The North Bridge over the Concord River has come to be known as "the rude bridge" from a descriptive phrase in *The Concord Hymn* composed by Ralph Waldo Emerson for the unveiling of the Battle Monument on April 19, 1836. You may remember the first quatrain:

> *By the rude bridge that arched the flood,*
> *Their flag to April's breeze unfurled,*
> *Here once the embattled farmers stood,*
> *And fired the shot heard round the world.*

In 1775 when the battle took place the bridge was approached by a road from the west which was abandoned in 1793. Since then there has been no western exit, and the bridge is a museum piece to mark the historic site. It carries the visitor to the screen of trees and hedges that make a setting for the statue of the Minute Man by Daniel Chester French.

The Americans on that morning of April 19 assembled on a hill to the northwest near Major John Buttrick's farmhouse. From this eminence they watched the British soldiers guarding the crossing, about a hundred of them, undetermined what to do. The decision came when they saw smoke rising from Concord village and mistook its meaning. "Will you let them burn the town down?" cried Joseph Hosmer, and then their line formed. They marched down the hill in column of twos, fifers shrilling *The White Cockade*, turned left, and now they faced the bridge—and the enemy.

As the Americans advanced steadily the British fired a volley, killing two and wounding others. The Americans returned the fire, killing and wounding a number of the British. There were three or four hundred Americans in the attack, and the British panicked before the superior force. They retreated in disorder and started up Monument Street to the center of the town. The Americans followed them a short distance, then broke off, and mounted a hill to take cover behind a stone wall.

The fight at Concord Bridge began and ended in minutes, but its impact would arouse a new nation.

38

WEDDING CAKE HOUSE—KENNEBUNK, MAINE

Just outside the village of Kennebunk the motorist will be startled to come upon this yellow brick, two-story house to which an astonishing icing of scroll-saw work has been added. For years it has been known as "the wedding-cake house." The structure seems to have been built in the early nineteenth century, but just when, and by whom, and more importantly, why this strange decoration was added, no one seems to know. The proportions of the original house are excellent, with a central doorway and a fine Palladian window above. The lacy scroll-saw work that has been affixed to the square mass gives a bizarre effect that is probably unmatched anywhere in the United States.

Kennebunk has a number of fine houses and traces its history back to 1630. Before the Revolution it was an important ship-building community with a flourishing West Indies trade, which brought wealth to its merchants and ship owners. It is situated on the Mousam River which runs down to the sea at Kennebunkport. It, too, was a ship-building center and a port of importance in Revolutionary days and after. It has some handsome houses that go back to 1785, and you will see above their gable or gambrel roofs a captain's walk. This was a small observation deck to which a ship owner, who had usually been a captain in his youth, climbed to scour the sea for a glimpse of the tall mast which meant that one of his ships was about to enter the harbor. All too frequently the ship never made port, and its fate was unknown. The captain's walk is sometimes called a widow's walk or even a widow's weep, for the wives sought this eyrie, too, gazing anxiously for the return of a husband who might never come home again.

FISHING SCENE—PROVINCETOWN, MASSACHUSETTS

Provincetown has been a commercial fishing center for nearly three hundred years. Its history begins far behind that, for on November 11, 1620, the *Mayflower* dropped anchor in the harbor, and the Pilgrims had the land of America under their feet at last. They remained here for five weeks and then sailed on to Plymouth.

This view is taken on the town wharf in spring. At the far end are tied up the boats of the commercial fishing fleet which discharge their cargoes into large warehouses where they are sorted, iced, and sent by refrigerator trucks to market cities. Along one side of the wharf are berths for the party and charter boats which carry out sports fishermen each day in spring, summer and autumn.

For years the town has been an artists' colony, and by now the flavor of the crowds—and the art—is quite avant garde As you cruise the two principal streets you find them lined with old houses, shops displaying a variety of merchandise, restaurants, and food stands. Here you may gorge yourself on steamed clams and other New England delicacies, including lobster roll. There are enough houses from Provincetown's great days to give you a feeling of what it was like before it was invaded by the modern wave.

A steamer used to come down from Boston every day, a pleasant three-hour sail. No more. There was also a line of the New Haven, but that long ago became a casualty of the motoring age. Buses are the only means of public transport today. There is a fine motoring road which will give you an idea of the still wild state of the Cape, once you are inland from the shore.

42

SILVER SHOP—OLD DEERFIELD, MASSACHUSETTS

This ancient town is a scene of tranquillity today under its great trees, hardly evoking the tragic memories of massacres which were committed in its first three decades by Indians and Frenchmen. It was settled in 1669, the farthest north village in the Province of Massachusetts Bay. The country was wilderness.

The first Indian raids took place in September, 1675, culminating in the Bloody Brook massacre in which sixty-four men of Deerfield were killed. The bereaved and bewildered survivors left the settlement, moving south to towns already established. By 1682 the colony was reestablished, the houses rebuilt, new and stronger stockades set up. There were only sporadic attacks until 1704 when, on February 29, a large force of French soldiers accompanied by Indians fell on the village just before daybreak. Of the 291 inhabitants, forty-eight were killed and 111 taken prisoner. These miserable captives were immediately started on the three-hundred-mile march to Canada.

A walk along mile-long Old Deerfield Street—usually called just The Street —finds it lined with Colonial houses, some quite fine, others more simple but all touched by the nostalgia of an earlier time. Some are open to the public, and one of these is the Silver Shop whose exterior is shown. The building had been moved out of town but in 1960 it was restored to its original site as the Parker and Russell Silver Shop. It has been handsomely restored, not only with furniture but with the tools of the silversmith's craft. It contains a fine collection of Colonial silver.

MUNROE TAVERN—LEXINGTON, MASSACHUSETTS

Built in 1695, the Munroe Tavern was already eighty years old on April 19, 1775, when the British marched out. It stands on the eastern outskirts of Lexington and had no part in the dawn attack by the regulars on the Americans stretched across Lexington Green. Its proprietor, William Munroe, a sergeant of Minute Men, was in the line with his friends and neighbors but was not struck by the three British volleys.

The tavern, now handsomely restored, comes into the picture on the afternoon of that day, about three o'clock, when Hugh Earl Percy, leading his relief force of about a thousand men, chose it as his headquarters. Percy was the son of the Duke of Northumberland and a fine soldier. In an expedition distinguished by blundering, he was cool and far-seeing. Anticipating that the Americans might have destroyed the bridge over the Charles River at Cambridge, he added carpenters to his force to repair any damage. He also had the foresight to bring along two light cannons.

Percy was right about the bridge. The Americans had taken up the planks but had not done a very good job. They were piled on the Cambridge side, and it was an easy matter for some of his men to cross on the stringers and put the planks in place. There was little delay, and the troops marched on to Lexington. Percy stopped his force opposite the Munroe Tavern, hearing the firing just ahead, and then opened his ranks. The Grenadiers and Light Infantry of the retreating British came into this sanctuary, so exhausted that they stretched out on the ground, their tongues lolling like dogs'. They were given half an hour to rest. Then Percy got them on their feet, formed both forces, and began the march back to Charlestown, where the boats were waiting.

HARRISON GRAY OTIS HOUSE—BEACON HILL, BOSTON

The great Boston architect, Charles Bulfinch, designed three grand houses for Harrison Gray Otis, and all three are still standing. The first, built in 1795–6, is at 141 Cambridge Street. Our photograph shows the second and much larger house constructed in 1800 on Beacon Hill at 85 Mount Vernon Street, next door to charming Louisburg Square (pronounced as though spelled "Lewisburg").

Otis and a syndicate of his friends had purchased most of Beacon Hill when it was pastureland. This house must have been one of the earliest. Within the next fifteen or twenty years the three principal streets—Beacon, Chestnut, and Mount Vernon—were lined with fine houses, and the Hill became the choice residential district of Boston.

In 1806 Otis moved again, this time to the house Bulfinch designed at 45 Beacon Street, and here he lived for the rest of his long life. "Harry" Otis, as he was called by his friends, was a most amiable and distinguished gentleman, a leader in the political, social, and legal life of Boston. Through wise speculation in local real estate, he added to his income from the law. By the time these three houses were built he was a wealthy man.

After serving in the General Court of Massachusetts, he was elected to Congress when Philadelphia was the national capital. He chose not to seek re-election but returned with his wife to Boston where they settled down as leaders of society. Otis had long since become Boston's favorite orator and he was also known as a gracious host and witty conversationalist, a perfect representative of Boston's Brahmins.

48

COVERED BRIDGE—TAFTSVILLE, VERMONT

Though covered bridges are thought by most to be indigenous to New England and very old, the first was erected over the Schuylkill River at Philadelphia in 1804. Many covered bridges were built in the next fifty years and with different structural designs. Alabama had sixty, Indiana 174, Kentucky thirty-five, Ohio 349, Pennsylvania 390, and Oregon 149. It is a common belief in the north that the covered bridge was designed only to protect the roadway from snow— and that was indeed one good reason—but there were others. One important reason was to keep water out of the joints, where it might freeze during the winter or cause rotting in summer. Another you might not think of was to give the structure a barnlike appearance, since farm animals did not relish crossing a rushing river and were likely to run and not walk, thereby shaking the structure. Of course covered bridges were built for the horse-and-buggy days and became virtually obsolete with the motor car and particularly the giant truck. They have been gradually replaced by more sturdy structures, though they remain on the byways as reminders of a gentle past.

Taftsville is not far from the charming town of Woodstock, long a summer resort and said to have built the first ski slope in New England. Before reaching Taftsville the motorist will have passed over—but stopped to marvel at— Quechee Gorge, a surprising and awesome wonder in the Vermont countryside. The highway bridge stands 165 feet above the floor of a wild, rocky gorge cut by the Ottauquechee River through countless time and still flowing as a slender stream at the bottom. It is a sight to remember.

JOHN BROWN HOUSE—PROVIDENCE, RHODE ISLAND

John Brown and his three brothers, Joseph, Nicholas, and Moses, were prosperous merchants and shipowners of Providence. They were also vigorous patriots in the years preceding the Revolution. In 1772, when the British revenue cutter *Gaspee* ran aground in Narragansett Bay in pursuit of the Providence packet, John Brown was the leader of a party of Providence men who boarded the vessel, took off its crew, and burned the cutter to the waterline.

The British in London, furious at this attack on a naval vessel, appointed a royal commission to seek out the perpetrators and to send those responsible to England to be tried for treason. The commission met the following January and again in May, but no single witness would be found to identify any of the burners of the *Gaspee*, though their identities must have been well known.

The John Brown house at 52 Power Street was designed by his brother Joseph, an amateur but inspired architect. It was begun in 1786 and two years in the building. Young John Quincy Adams described it in 1789 as the most magnificent and elegant mansion he had seen in this country, and perhaps that was an understatement. It is three stories in height, almost square in mass, with a central pavilion and pediment built of red brick and sandstone, a fine balustraded parapet above the cornice. Over the doorway is a Palladian window with elaborate leaded side lights. The building is a gem of late Georgian architecture with beautiful interiors and furnishings. This view, taken in spring, gives a rich prospect of the noble house.

Summer

MYSTIC SEAPORT—CONNECTICUT

Tied up to a wharf, the stern of the veteran whaler *Charles W. Morgan* is the most fascinating exhibit of Mystic Seaport, a restored village on the Connecticut shore beyond New London, dedicated to perpetuating the maritime glory of the nineteenth century. The museum of nearly sixty buildings was the dream of three prominent citizens of Mystic, who founded the Marine Historical Association in 1929. Since then their endeavor has been widely supported, both by generous donations and by thousands of visitors who come each year to see what has grown to a fabulous collection of ships, ship-building crafts at work, and hundreds of fully rigged models.

The *Morgan* was built in 1841 at Fairhaven, next door to New Bedford, Massachusetts. Her mainmast rises 110 feet above the deck, and when fully rigged the ship would carry 33,000 square feet of canvas. For eighty years the *Morgan* chased whales in all waters. Nearby is the *Bowdoin*, which Rear Admiral Donald B. MacMillan skippered on twenty-six voyages of exploration into Arctic waters. As a young man, MacMillan sailed with Rear Admiral Robert E. Peary on the 1909 expedition when Peary reached the North Pole. He never turned his back on Arctic seas. Another stout veteran is the *Joseph Conrad*, a square rigger which was over many years a training ship for cadets of the Danish navy. One fascinating exhibit is a ropewalk where the skill of making rope for ships is carried on as it has been for thousands of years. Formerly these long buildings were a part of every ship-building community, but it would be hard to find one at work today—except at Mystic.

54

WHITCOMB HOUSE—HANCOCK, NEW HAMPSHIRE

Hancock is a lovely village in the southwestern part of the state not far from Nashua. The Whitcomb house has a peculiar interest. It was built by two brothers, John and Henry Whitcomb, in 1812 as a "twin" house. It has brick ends and a double door in the center which opens to twin but quite separate apartments. The brothers, married at Christmastime, brought their brides here together. Even the furnishings of the two halves of the house are identical, and the families are said to have lived here happily for many years.

The brothers operated a general store next door. John, who seems to have been the more aggressive of the two, was postmaster for twenty-eight years and a choir singer for forty. Hancock was settled in 1764 when John Grimes built a cabin on Half-Moon Pond. The town received a charter in 1769 and was named "Hancock" in honor of John Hancock of Massachusetts, one of the nonresident owners of the town. Hancock took no interest in his holding, as far as is known, but he was an eminent man, and the town rejoiced in his distant aura. For a time it was a place of some manufacturing importance with cotton mills and tanneries. These were abandoned long ago, and it is now a village again with a broad main street, arched by trees, and lived in by families who love New Hampshire.

HOUSE OF SEVEN GABLES—SALEM, MASSACHUSETTS

This is undoubtedly the most famous house in Salem, though by no means the equal in architectural beauty of the fine flowering of late eighteenth-century and early nineteenth-century houses, many of them designed or inspired by the great local architect, Samuel McIntire. The House of Seven Gables was built at the water's edge in 1668 by Captain John Turner. Three generations of the Turner family lived here, and in 1782 it was sold to the Ingersoll family. The fame of the old house springs largely from the fact that Nathaniel Hawthorne took it as the model in his novel, *The House of Seven Gables*. The house was restored in 1910 and attracts thousands of visitors each year.

The glory of Salem lies in its maritime past and the great town houses. It was the China trade which turned Salem's greatest profit. In 1785 its first China-bound ship, the *Grand Turk*, sailed out and soon a fleet of thirty-four vessels had been put on the China run by Salem shipowners and captains. These were not direct round-trip voyages. The ships stopped at ports along the way where they might sell all or part of their cargoes, taking on other merchandise. They came home around the Cape of Good Hope, often stopping in European ports for a bit of trading. On many of these voyages they had turned over their cargoes many times, and their profits soared. Then the great houses were assured.

One quite different exhibition Salem has to offer is the Pioneers' Village which shows what the town was like in 1630 at the beginning of its history, with bark-covered wigwams of the sort in which the settlers first lived.

NUBBLE LIGHT—YORK HARBOR, MAINE

On an island outside York Harbor Nubble Light must have caused the brushes of hundreds of Sunday painters to twitch until they had it on canvas. It is a beauty, as is its twin on Boon Island nearby. York Harbor has long been an exclusive resort with estates and residences built along heavily shaded streets. York Beach is a resort area with public facilities but still quiet and pleasant. Long Beach, which is part of the York Beach resort, has cottages bordering the shore road. It is a wide beach, unmarred by concessions, and a delight to bathers who can take the somewhat chilly temperatures of Maine summer waters.

The motoring family would have a marvelous time cruising the coast of Maine and stopping at these long sandy beaches. Old Orchard, which is above Kennebunk but below Portland, is one of the finest beaches in America, extending back from the sea. It is so big that you will hardly notice the hamburger stands and such until you are glad to patronize them yourself.

This has been Maine vacation country for decades. Families have taken shore-side houses and children have grown up—boys and girls—to learn sailing from their fathers. They have been seated with a tiller in small catboats to race with their peers and absorb a taste of the sea which will never leave them. In their fifties and sixties they can step into a ketch or a yawl and guide it brilliantly over a twenty-mile course. This is New England, where any son or daughter learns when the sail is luffing to turn into or away from the wind. It is something bred into children, following their salt-water ancestors, and what a lovely thing it is! They may never sail around the Horn but perhaps they could. Their ancestors did. Perhaps they would!

60

SHORT HOUSE—OLD NEWBURY, MASSACHUSETTS

Newbury, now usually called Old Newbury, was the first settlement in this area, dating from 1635. The settlers spent seven dreary years trying to practice agriculture in the forests and then moved to the mouth of the Merrimack where they established Newburyport. Newbury was not abandoned, however, and old houses remain there, one of the finest being the Short House which dates from 1773. It is a two-story structure with gabled brick ends, red trim, and clapboards which have long since weathered to a mellow dark brown. The interior woodwork in two of the rooms is notable. Paint has been removed from the paneling to reveal skillful carving in the full-length pilasters which flank the fireplaces. The house is set against a backdrop of fine trees.

In Newburyport next door the visitor will find one of the most flavorsome cities in New England. Its shipping once rivaled Boston's, and the tall houses that line High Street are a reminder of its affluence. In the nineteenth century its yards saw the launching of clipper ships designed by the great naval architect, Donald McKay. Among the most interesting—and finest—houses on High Street is the one built by Lord Timothy Dexter in 1771. The title was of his own invention, and he rightly described himself as an eccentric. He based his fortune on buying up depreciated Continental currency and holding it until the nation was on a sounder standard. He also engaged in strange shipping ventures, the most noted being to send a cargo of warming pans to the West Indies. To the discomfiture of his laughing critics, they found an immediate market—as ladles for the islands' most important export, molasses.

62

HARBOR AND CRUISE SHIPS—CAMDEN, MAINE

Overlooking Penobscot Bay, Camden is one of the loveliest towns in Maine. Its generous and safe harbor lies below the steep heights of the Penobscot Range, which have attracted skiers for thirty years and, with the sailing in summer, have given this resort town a year-round life. Hardy souls also climb the hills for the magnificent top-side views of the Bay. On his 1614 survey of the coast Captain John Smith took special, and somewhat poetical, note of this location, lying "under the high mountains of the Penobscot, against whose feet the sea doth beat."

Many summer vacationers go to Camden to take fishing cruises with Yankee skippers. Their boats are clean and comfortable, and such a cruise makes an unusual and exciting vacation. Both men and women singles have done this, and it is an excellent way for young people to get together.

Camden is a favoured harbor for yachts coasting down to Maine to anchor for a night or two with a restful sense of security, particularly when the fogs blow in as they do in August. You are safe here, safe, to remember a New England expression, "as you'd be in God's pocket." And it is a charming place to linger. Behind the Public Library is an amphitheatre and there is the old Camden Opera House, remodeled thirty years ago into a modern auditorium with tasteful interior decoration. Camden is not big and noisy but small and restful and dignified. With the great harbor overlooking Penobscot Bay and the Camden Hills above, it is a place to stay quietly and enjoy deeply for the remembrance of what Maine is and has always been.

LAFAYETTE HOUSE—MARBLEHEAD, MASSACHUSETTS

The house facing you has nothing to do with Lafayette himself but everything to do with his carriage. On his triumphal tour of America in 1824 the great Frenchman spent the night in more fine houses than even the great number that boast "George Washington slept here." When Lafayette was approaching Marblehead the town fathers were worried that his grand coach could never turn the corner shown here. According to the legend a part of the house was cut away so the carriage could pass. With the narrow streets of Marblehead, traffic still has a hard time making this turn.

Marblehead was settled in 1629 by a hard-bitten crew from Cornwall and the Channel Islands as a plantation of Salem. They quickly gathered a reputation as a hard-drinking, roistering lot of fishermen. But they quietened down in time, and Marblehead began a more serious life, sending its ships to the West Indies and other ports. Prosperity came, and great houses rose.

During the Revolution Marblehead's General John Glover (who was a sailor rather than an army man) organized an "amphibious regiment" which, among many actions, ferried General Washington and his men across the Delaware River for the successful Christmas attack on the Hessian garrison at Trenton.

The Victorian Town Hall and Public Library, Abbot Hall, has the famous Willard painting, "The Spirit of '76," which shows three generations on the march, a grandfather, son, and grandson. One is a fifer, two are drummers, and we can assume they are playing *Yankee Doodle*. Let us admit that it is not a great painting but it has inspired Americans for a great many years.

66

FISHING FLEET—GLOUCESTER, MASSACHUSETTS

For well over three hundred years Gloucester on Cape Ann has maintained the most active fishing fleet in New England. The Cape was first settled in 1624 and grew into a fishing community. The fleet goes to the Grand Banks but sometimes fishes closer to shore. For many years it was Yankees who manned the ships. More recently Italians, Portuguese, and Scandinavians have taken over the bulk of the trade. Overlooking the harbor stands a great bronze figure of the Gloucester Fisherman, memorial to the ten thousand men who are estimated to have been drowned in this hazardous business during the past three centuries. On an August Sunday afternoon a memorial service is held beside the Fisherman, and the names of those are read who have died in the past year. Flowers are cast on the sea in their memory.

Like any old town, Gloucester is one of narrow streets and old buildings. You will know it by the smell, a compound of tar, salt air, and the fresh aroma of codfish drying in the sun. Despite the smell there are summer resorts all around, and just beside Gloucester is Rockport. Both these towns have for years been artists' colonies. The scenes will tempt color cameras, too.

There are many interesting buildings and old houses but none to compare with those in some other places, for Gloucester was never a merchant's town. Its livelihood was from the fisheries, and a hazardous life, indeed. Still, it goes on, as it has always gone on, the earliest occupation that civilization—and precivilization—have known.

68

WHITEHALL—MIDDLETOWN, RHODE ISLAND

This house has an interesting history, for it was occupied by the English divine and philosopher, the Reverend George Berkeley, Dean of Derry and later Bishop of Cloyne in Ireland. Though he was born in Ireland, his parents and ancestry were English. The Dean conceived the project of founding a school in Bermuda for the training of colonials in the ministry, who would then become missionaries to the Indians. He set out with his wife in September, 1728, but his captain badly missed Bermuda and ended up at Newport in January, 1729.

Dean Berkeley decided to remain in Newport and bought a seventeenth-century farmhouse in Middletown to the north of Newport on the Island of Rhode Island. He remodeled and enlarged it to the handsome structure that appears here in summer dress. It is now operated by the Colonial Dames who rescued it from decay and, with fine furnishings of the period, it is open to the public.

Only two years after his arrival, the Dean learned that the English government would not support the school he had hoped to found, so he returned home. But before leaving the colony—then known as the Colony of Rhode Island and Providence Plantations—he gave his considerable library of 880 volumes to Yale College as well as the deed to Whitehall, which he had named in honor of the royal residence in Whitehall Street, London. The rent of the house provided funds for a scholarship at Yale known as "the Dean's Bounty."

MEETING HOUSE—CASTINE, MAINE

The Old Meeting House, looking out over the village green, dates from 1790 and is one of the oldest in Maine. Castine had a stirring history in Colonial times, changing hands repeatedly over the years in a seesaw struggle between the British and French. It was attacked by Indians and once by the Dutch. Beginning in 1700 it had a period of peace until, in the Revolutionary War, the British occupied it in 1779. It was one of the few instances when the war came to New England.

The Americans determined to raid the place, and Paul Revere, by now an army colonel, had a command with the militia. A strong fleet was assembled, but the entire expedition was botched, chiefly through rivalry between army and navy units. There were delays in pressing the attack until the urgent appeals of the British garrison at Castine brought warships from New York which scattered the American flotilla.

The Americans melted into the forests along the Penobscot River to make their way on foot back to Boston. Revere was accused of cowardice and of failing to obey orders, and for years he pressed demands for a court martial so he could answer the charges. Finally it took place, and he was fully cleared by the court, the general judgment being that in the confusion following the Castine disaster it would have been impossible for anyone to obey orders and there was no evidence of cowardice.

That was a long time ago, and now Castine is a charming summer colony with old houses to be seen as well as points of historic interest. There is a flavor about this old town which stays with the visitor.

GEORGE STREET—PROVIDENCE, RHODE ISLAND

George Street runs parallel with Brown University at the top of College Hill, continuing down the slope until it meets Benefit Street. Brown was originally established at Warren as Rhode Island College, with a charter stipulating freedom of conscience for all students. In 1770 it was moved to an eight-acre eminence in Providence. With the beginning of the Revolution college activities were suspended, and American—later French—troops were quartered here. After the war the college curriculum was resumed and, in 1804, the name was changed to Brown University in gratitude to Nicholas Brown who had endowed a chair of Oratory and Belles Lettres. Pembroke College for women, which has the same faculty, was founded in 1819.

College Hill and the slopes below it comprise the old residential district of Providence. Our summer view looks down George Street with the buildings of modern Providence in the distance. The John Brown house is nearby, and on the streets that criss-cross the hill, particularly Benefit Street, there are many houses and other buildings that date from Colonial times or the early nineteenth century when men like the four Brown brothers were thriving merchants and ship owners. Roger Williams' house stood at the base of the hill on North Main Street, and his grave is behind the Sullivan Dorr house on Benefit Street, part of his original property.

The elegance of some of the historic houses is a fair indication of the prosperity that Providence enjoyed as early as the middle of the eighteenth century. The wonder is that so many of them remain.

74

Autumn

COUNTRY STORE—WILTON, CONNECTICUT

In spite of the prevalence of supermarkets and shopping centers, the country store is still a familiar sight in New England. Their exteriors are most colorful in fall, as this view shows, when the harvest has contributed piles of apples, pumpkins, and winter squash, vegetables and fruits whose colors match the brilliance of the autumn foliage. If you wander inside you may find almost anything, for these country merchants supply the needs of the locals. In addition to groceries, meats, and drugs you are apt to see a bewildering conglomeration of hardware, grass seed and fertilizers for the fall rejuvenation of summer-parched lawns, motorized mowers that convert to snow-removal duties in the cold months, sporting equipment, sleds and tricycles.

The antique shop in the background of the photograph is a reminder that the New England countryside is dotted with these purveyors of tables, chairs, and other furniture as well as china and glassware from earlier times. The shops vary in size a great deal but, big or small, they are fun to visit, and the chances are that you will find something that you would like to take home, even though it is no more than a pretty cupless saucer to place on a living-room table as an ash-tray.

Wilton, which lies on the perimeter of New York's commuting area, still gives the appearance of being unhurried and venerable. It is not far from Stamford and inland from the parkways and thruways which carry traffic at sixty-mile-an-hour speed to New Haven and beyond to Providence, Boston, the Cape, and north into New Hampshire, Vermont, and Maine.

MIDDLE STREET—PORTSMOUTH, NEW HAMPSHIRE

A visit to Portsmouth leaves no doubt that this is a seaport town with a rich history from Colonial days. Its fine houses speak of fortunes made there in the years of sail, when Portsmouth, like other New England seaports, sent its ships over the oceans to trade with cities on every continent. Its winding narrow streets with their great trees still tell of the town's past glory.

The photograph, taken in early autumn, gives a glimpse of the dignified dwellings that line Middle Street. The Langley-Boardman house, in the foreground, was built about 1805. It has a graceful Ionic portico surmounted by a Palladian window of great delicacy. The front door is of solid mahogany, and its oval panels are edged in whalebone. In the middle distance is Samuel Larkin's white house and beyond it, the brick mansion he built, now known as the Larkin-Rice house. Larkin made a fortune as auctioneer of British vessels taken by privateersmen in the War of 1812. He was also the father of twenty-two children, and this considerable family outgrew the first house.

Portsmouth has so many fine houses that it is impossible to mention them here, but a visit to the town will easily locate the most interesting. In the Piscataqua River lies Portsmouth Navy Yard on a number of islands which rightfully belong to Kittery, Maine, just across. The yard dates back to 1794. A more recent historical note is that President Theodore Roosevelt selected it for meetings of the council to draw up peace terms after the Russo-Japanese War. The Treaty of Portsmouth was signed there on September 5, 1905.

78

VILLAGE COMMON—NORWICH, VERMONT

Norwich lies just across the river from Hanover, New Hampshire, and is a favorite residential spot for Dartmouth College faculty. No wonder, for it is an ideal New England village, and the Common shown here in fall splendor is perfection for what it compactly includes. The town offices, the church, and the school are all in the view, and it is rare that such a picture can be made as this autumn scene along the Connecticut River.

The village rests under a thick foliage of maples, green in summer, but with autumn they have turned the deep red which makes the maples a spectacular part of autumn's display. Old frame houses lie behind white picket fences, and the village is every bit an incarnation of what New England has been from its years of the past.

This section of Vermont and New Hampshire on both sides of the Connecticut River is a place to enjoy. On the Vermont side is a fine river scene with the broad stream flowing smoothly between gently curved banks. It is the sort of view to be found all through rural New England where history goes back to the mid-eighteenth century.

On the New Hampshire side is Dartmouth, and this is a place so advanced from the year 1769 when it was founded by Eleazer Wheelock "to teach the In-di-an," as the old college song has it, that you will be astonished to find what it now offers the student body and visitors. The old buildings are beautiful and mellow, the new ones in harmony, and the experience will leave you with a feeling of pride in what imagination can do in broadening the opportunities of a modern college.

THE WAYSIDE INN—SOUTH SUDBURY, MASSACHUSETTS

To visit the Wayside Inn is one of New England's rich experiences, for this tavern on the Post Road from Boston goes back to 1686 when it was opened by Samuel Howe. Originally known as Howe's Tavern, Samuel's grandson, Ezekiel, changed its name to the Red Horse Tavern in 1746. The sign with its prancing red horse still hangs as advertisement and invitation. The tavern passed from father to son until 1860, when the last Howe died, a bachelor, and it ceased being an inn until 1896 when the property was once more opened to the public for food, lodging, and refreshment.

It was Henry Wadsworth Longfellow who lifted the ancient hostelry from its local prestige when he published his *Tales of a Wayside Inn* in 1863. He planned this collection of poems somewhat in the manner of Chaucer's *Canterbury Tales*, with a group of seven friends sitting around the fireplace of the tavern's living room, each telling a story, and Longfellow describing the place himself in affectionate memory.

In 1923 Henry Ford bought the Wayside Inn and restored it, hunting out some of the Howe furnishings that had disappeared and contributing others which fitted the Colonial heritage of the ancient tavern. He also acquired old buildings from the vicinity, bought more land, and moved them to the property so that today a leisurely visit with a lunch or dinner is something to remember. One of the buildings is the small schoolhouse which is celebrated in "Mary had a little lamb."

82

SQUAM LAKE—NEW HAMPSHIRE

In this photograph the serenity of autumn falls about Squam Lake Inlet. The summer residents have gone, their fine houses left to caretakers, and the big lake with its twenty-six islands "goes native," prepared for another winter of ice and snow. Squam lies near, and slightly northwestward of Lake Winnipesaukee, the big one that is twenty-two miles in length with a width varying from one to ten miles.

Squam Lake has been a summer-resort community since the 1870s and, while much smaller than Winnipesaukee, is much of a lake. On its shores lies the town of Holderness, established after the defeat of the French at Quebec in 1759, with the thought that the danger of Indian attacks was now ended, for this was very much Indian territory. The grant of a township was made by the Royal Governor to Major John Wentworth and a group of English emigrants who were devout communicants of the Anglican Church. Strangely, the colonists built a rosy future for their settlement, predicting that it would become the foremost town in New England, dwarfing the prominence of Boston.

The lake is surrounded by high green hills and richly forested shores. In the distance the bare and rugged peak of Mt. Chocorua rises, and the whole setting is one of primeval glory, in spite of the summer homes that are back from the lake. To drive around it in autumn is almost to ignore these modern incursions on the ancient woodlands which come down to the shores of the lovely lake. To be sure there is swimming, boating, and fishing, but the landscape is so vast in this quarter of New Hampshire that the intruders are hardly noticed. They could be still the Indians in their bark canoes.

OLD NORTH CHURCH—BOSTON, MASSACHUSETTS

The proper name is Christ Church, and it was built in 1723. Its faith is Anglican, and it was the first church in Boston to possess a pleasant peal of eight bells. It stands in Boston's North End and it was the northernmost of that quarter's several churches, the others built around North Square where Paul Revere had his house and silversmith's shop. Of them all, the building of Christ Church alone survives.

The historical fame of the Old North Church rests on its claim that on the night of April 18, 1775, two lanterns were hung in the tower to warn the anxious watchers in Charlestown that the British troops were coming out—"by sea." This meant they would be ferried in boats to East Cambridge from which they would begin their march to Lexington and Concord. In his poem, *The Midnight Ride of Paul Revere*, Longfellow has Revere himself in Charlestown watching for the lights. This is incorrect. Revere was in Boston where he remained till the British plans were fully disclosed. Then he instructed a friend—possibly the sexton—to show two lanterns and went down to the shore from which he was rowed to Charlestown. The previous Sunday he had arranged to have a watch set there each night, and if the signal appeared a rider was to be sent immediately to warn Lexington and Concord.

Visiting the Old North provides some emotional realizations of history, for the interior is as it was when the Bostonians knelt there in the first quarter of the eighteenth century, following the prayer book their fathers had known in the Mother Country. Below the church is a crypt which may be visited. Among the burials is that of Major John Pitcairn, who led the British Light Infantry onto Lexington Green. He was killed two months later at the Battle of Bunker Hill.

WHITE MOUNTAINS—NEW HAMPSHIRE

Nowhere in New England is the autumn foliage more spectacular than in the White Mountains. A circuit by car in late September or early October leaves unforgettable memories of its brilliance. With color film a record may be made that would seem unbelievable if you traversed the same route in spring or summer. A tour of the White Mountains will bring you not only to Mt. Washington but in sight of the Presidential Range running in a double curve from northeast to southwest. The principal peaks are Mt. Madison, Mt. Adams, Mt. Jefferson, and Mt. Clay, all more than 5000 feet above sea level but lower than Mt. Washington's 6288 feet.

Darby Field, the first white man to ascend Mt. Washington, made the climb in the company of two Indians in 1642. It was two centuries later when the way was made easier. A carriage road was engineered and opened in 1861. In 1869 the cog railway was put in operation, and this is still the most effortless way to get to the top. The carriage road, eight miles long, took automobiles as soon as the motor car was capable of making the ascent. First up was a Stanley Steamer around the turn of the century.

Scenery throughout the White Mountains is magnificent in any season with alternating peaks and deep valleys and "notches." From Franconia Notch you will get the best view of that astonishing profile—"the old man of the mountain" or, as he has been also called, "the great stone face."

Winter

PARSON CAPEN HOUSE—TOPSFIELD, MASSACHUSETTS

The town of Topsfield granted land to its new parson, the Reverend Joseph Capen, in 1682, in a field adjacent to the old white church. The parson's bride, who came from the prominent Appleton family in nearby Ipswich, wanted a new and more important parsonage, and a replica of an English manor house of the period was erected in 1683, overlooking gentle meadows and surrounded by pleasant woods.

The house has the typical second-story overhang of Elizabethan architecture, supported by hewn brackets above the front door on either side. Had it been built in England, instead of the clapboards it would undoubtedly have been constructed in the half-timbered style which caused these buildings to be known as "black and white" houses from the weathered black of the oak beams against the daub and plaster between them.

The interior here is built around a great central chimney, the usual design of early Colonial houses. Though most of the seventeenth-century furnishings have been assembled since the house became a museum piece, its fireplaces, stair rail, and newel post are original, and its essential character has not been altered. The leanto, so often added later in such houses, was also part of the basic plan.

The Parson Capen house is one of the gems of early Colonial architecture in New England. The parson and his bride never parted from the view. They lie side by side in a hillside burying ground not far away.

STREET SCENE—MARBLEHEAD, MASSACHUSETTS

This charming corner of Marblehead is known as Glover Court, from the house of General John Glover which stands at the right of the photograph. To the left is the Norden House, a hardy survivor from the seventeenth century. General Glover was a seaman rather than a soldier, but he was effective in both arms of the service. He established an amphibious force which ferried the defeated colonials from Brooklyn to Manhattan after the disastrous battle of Long Island. Following the loss of Fort Washington his boats carried the troops across the Hudson. He was active throughout the early years of hostilities, serving in the campaign that ended in the massive British defeat at Saratoga in October 1777. But certainly his most memorable service was in ferrying the troops of General Washington over the ice-clogged Delaware River for the attack on Trenton, New Jersey, at Christmas 1776.

A ramble through Marblehead will bring the visitor to many fine houses. On Washington Street stand the Colonel William Lee and Jeremiah Lee residences. On Hooper Street is the King Hooper house, built in 1748 by Robert Hooper, whose nickname of "King" came not only from his great wealth but from his royal manner of life. Back on Washington Street again is the house of Elbridge Gerry. Gerry, a lusty patriot, was Vice President of the United States under James Madison in the War of 1812. Previously, as Governor of Massachusetts, he is credited with the device of laying out election districts so they would be safe for the party in power. The word "gerrymander" was coined for this type of tinkering, since the resulting districts often took the tortuous shape of a salamander.

CHRISTMAS ON THE FARM—ESSEX, MASSACHUSETTS

This photograph seems to evoke many memories of what the ideal Christmas setting should be—a farmhouse blanketed with snow and waiting for the children and grandchildren. You can almost imagine the big sleigh drawing up, the buffalo robes thrown aside as the youngsters leap out and rush to the front door to be greeted with yuletide hugs. It was a scene repeated all over New England for countless years.

Now the unloading of the gaily wrapped presents while the team is led, nostrils steaming, to the barn, and the reunion in the house is complete, with old memories crowding up in the familiar surroundings. Later the family will say there never *was* such a Christmas, but tonight after dinner they will read *A Christmas Carol* and, before the nodding children are carried to bed, *A Visit from St. Nicholas*. Then the grown-ups, old and young, will cluster around the fire with a pitcher of mulled wine on the hob or perhaps glasses of hot buttered rum all around.

These country Christmases were times to remember—for the younger ones as they took the children home, for the grandparents who remained in the big house with memories that would not fade. It was a time for contemplation. The country was dormant under its mantle of snow. It was the end of another year. A new one lay just ahead, and in those years of the nineteenth century it would carry on the warm, safe, comfortable living of the past.

This is the essence of New England.

94